Original title:
The Purpose of Life Is... Wait, What Was I Saying?

Copyright © 2025 Creative Arts Management OÜ
All rights reserved.

Author: Rosalie Bradford
ISBN HARDBACK: 978-1-80566-048-4
ISBN PAPERBACK: 978-1-80566-343-0

Clarity in a Misty Horizon

In the morning haze, I ponder still,
Sipping coffee, searching for a thrill.
A sock's missing, where did it go?
My quest for meaning fuels the show.

Maps of thoughts in a jumbled mess,
Navigating life, I must confess.
Is that a squirrel with a secret task?
Or am I just afraid to ask?

Threads of Meaning Unspooled

Tangled yarn on the living room floor,
What's life about? I can't quite score.
A cat stares back, judging my plight,
While I'm wrestling with cosmic insight.

Do we knit with purpose or just for fun?
Does the universe care? Or have I spun?
With every stitch, does clarity bloom?
Or do I just end up with a tangled room?

In Search of the Elusive Answer

Chasing shadows the whole day through,
My brain's a circus with no clear cue.
Did I feed the cat? Or was that a dream?
Questions pop up like a bad ice cream.

With every step, a new thought's found,
Like bubble gum stuck to the ground.
I trip and tumble on this quest,
Trying to find what makes life best.

The Tangle of Human Thought

In a maze of musings, I roam around,
Is this profound? Or just silly sound?
Friends laugh as I scratch my head,
Was I talking about cheese or the thread?

Doodles on napkins hold secrets deep,
As I ponder while others just sleep.
Snippets of wisdom float like confetti,
Yet here I am, still unsteady.

The Language of Wandering Hearts

In cities bright, we chase the sun,
Yet trip on dreams, oh what a fun!
With every wrong turn, laughter blooms,
As we dance 'round fate's strange rooms.

A cup of coffee, a slice of pie,
We ponder deep questions, oh my!
Then lose our thoughts, with snack in hand,
And giggle at our clueless stand.

Fragments of a Wayward Dream

A paper boat on a fishy stream,
Sails on whispers of a half-baked dream.
We chase the stars, yet fumble on ground,
What was that thought? It spun around.

In socks that mismatch and shoes untied,
We question the moon, then ask why we cried.
The answers hide in our messy hair,
Stuck in the fridge? Wait, there they were!

Uncharted Territories of Thought

Oh wanderlust! You cheeky guest,
We chart a map, forget the quest.
With snack breaks frequent, giggles loud,
Life's maze confounds us, what a crowd!

Between the lines, we lose our way,
A squirrel steals time, as we play.
What did I need? Whatever it was,
It slipped away, like unplayed fuzz.

Hues of Understanding and Forgetting

With crayons drawn on the walls of thought,
We sketch our hopes, but forget a lot.
A bouquet of wishes, a jumbled rhyme,
Who knew the clock would jump like time?

Between the giggles, a wisdom sprouts,
But falls like leaves when laughter shouts.
We scribble notes, we scribble fast,
Until the meaning's just a blast!

The Labyrinth of Lost Conversations

I wandered in my mind today,
Thoughts like mazes led astray.
Chasing shadows, laughing loud,
Caught in giggles, lost in crowd.

Ideas float on puffy clouds,
Silly whispers joke aloud.
Oh! What was that I meant to say?
Never mind, we'll laugh anyway.

Trails of Thought Like Fallen Leaves

Fallen thoughts like leaves in fall,
Scattered stories, can't recall.
A punchline hiding in the breeze,
Is that wisdom or just tease?

Every twist is just a giggle,
Mighty truths dissolve and wriggle.
What was I planning? Who can tell?
Lost again in thought's hotel.

An Odyssey of Incomplete Thoughts

A journey starts without a clue,
Half a notion, just a few.
Stumbling over awkward lines,
In this dance of silly signs.

Where was I? Oh, here I am,
Chasing thoughts in a wild jam.
Wait, what was I trying to prove?
Never mind, just keep the groove.

Distant Echoes of Lost Intentions

I had a plan, or maybe not,
Intentions drifting on the spot.
Echoes laughing from afar,
Tell me, where did I leave my car?

Reflections bouncing, what a sight,
Confusion reigns in broad daylight.
Oh, that thought, it slipped away,
Guess I'll just invent a game to play.

The Enigma of a Disoriented Soul

Was it breakfast or lunch, I can't tell,
The cat's in the cupboard, oh what a spell.
Did I sprinkle some wisdom on my toast?
Or just serve confusion like a gracious host?

Puzzles and riddles, they dance in my head,
Every thought sounds better when whispered in bread.
Should I call up my thoughts, or let them run free?
A game of charades with a side of caffeine.

Between Dreams and Distraction

I dreamt I was soaring on a bright blue kite,
But woke to my socks missing, what a fright!
There's a circus in my brain, juggling away,
While I search for a reason to start off my day.

My coffee cup whispers sweet secrets to me,
Yet all I can grasp are the stains on my tee.
The clock ticks in riddles, I can't seem to care,
Oh look, there's a squirrel—wait, what's in the air?

A Jigsaw of Half-remembered Moments

Pieces of laughter fall under my chair,
Hints of a memory float lingered in air.
Did I have a toast, or was it a dance?
I think it involved a very small chance.

I lost my old self in a pile of to-do,
A list full of 'maybe,' and 'not in the queue.'
Each step feels like falling, but I laugh as I go,
At the puzzle of life that may never quite show.

In the Theater of a Wandering Mind

A spotlight shines bright on my scattered thoughts,
Is that me on stage? Or a jumble of knots?
The audience chuckles at my comedic plight,
As I fumble and tumble, what's wrong and what's right?

My script's full of riddles, each line's a surprise,
Distant echoes of laughter dance in my eyes.
But the finale is near, and I'm still on my toes,
What was the punchline? Nobody knows!

Navigating Through the Fog

In a maze of thoughts I wander,
Lost amid the swirling haze,
A cat's tail flicks, I ponder,
What was I considering these days?

Laughter echoes in the mist,
Like a clown without a nose,
I chase the ideas on my list,
But where they go, nobody knows.

Whirlwinds of Reflections

A thought jumps like a spark,
Dancing wildly in the dark,
Like socks that vanish in the wash,
What did I intend? Oh, it's a nosh!

I scribble words, they fly away,
Chasing them leads to dismay,
Perhaps I'll nap, then try again,
Or just deny I'm in the pen!

A Mosaic of Momentary Insights

Pieces scattered, thoughts collide,
Like confetti in the breeze,
I search for meaning, then I hide,
Each whim with giggles brought to knees.

In a kaleidoscope of glee,
I spot a thought, it starts to twirl,
But, wait, was that a bumblebee?
Or just a thought that made me swirl?

The Journey of Unspoken Questions

Questions hover like a kite,
Tangled up, lost in flight,
Do I need to ask or know,
Why my sandwich fell below?

With a chuckle, I embrace,
The randomness that fills this space,
Life's a riddle, so amusing,
And half the time, it's just confusing!

Searching for Sense in Absurdity

In a world where logic plays hide and seek,
I ponder the meaning, but all I hear is bleak.
Waffles are wise, of that I am sure,
Yet chips on my shoulder beg for a cure.

I search under rocks and behind silly masks,
For answers to questions that no one but asks.
The sky laughs above, a jester in blue,
As I trip over thoughts like a clown at the zoo.

Trapped in a Cycle of Thoughts

Round and round like a merry-go-round,
My brain spins tales that make no sound.
Coffee's my friend, or so I would swear,
But caffeine just adds to the whimsical flair.

I talk to my plants; they nod and agree,
Yet here I am, stuck in this endless spree.
Have I left the oven on? Is that a cat?
Maybe it's time to sit down and chat.

Layers of Consciousness and Confusion

With layers of thoughts like an onion's skin,
I peel back the jokes to where I begin.
A sandwich from yesterday still brings me glee,
Yet I'm searching for wisdom inside of a flea.

Love is a riddle wrapped tight in a sock,
While socks without partners just wander and mock.
I scribble my musings on napkins and walls,
But soon they dissolve like my mental brawls.

Reverie in the Chaotic Unknown

In the chaos of dreams where logic goes wild,
I chase after thought, like a roaming child.
Is that a balloon or a thought taking flight?
Nope, just my head, bobbing left and right.

Thoughts jump like frogs on a sunlit pond,
While I search for a reason to carry on fond.
Each moment is silly, a jewel in the mess,
Draped in absurdity, I must confess.

The Rhythm of Ambiguous Thoughts

In a haze of coffee, I muse,
The toaster pops, but I've lost my clues.
A sock on the floor might hold the key,
To the great mystery of who to be.

Thoughts dancing around like a wily cat,
Chasing shadows, imagine that!
I scribble down quotes, they just don't stick,
And ponder the meaning of a rubber brick.

Glimpses of a Hidden Compass

Maps are for those who know the way,
But I prefer surprises to brighten my day.
Is it north or south, I can't quite decide,
With a compass that spins like it's trying to hide.

X marks the spot on a pizza slice,
But finding my wallet? Now, that's precise!
A treasure chest full of forgotten dreams,
My head is a fog; or so it seems.

Thoughts That Flutter Like Butterflies

Bright ideas flit like fragile wings,
Mimicking joy in the goofy things.
A glimpse of brilliance lost in a laugh,
While searching for meaning in my bath.

Sipping on tea while the world goes by,
Wondering if frogs ever learn to fly.
Jots and doodles all over my page,
If only wisdom came at that age.

The Curious Case of Wandering Ideas

Ideas roam like puppies in a park,
Sniffing around, leaving their mark.
One moment I'm deep in philosophical thought,
Next, it's about finding my last bag of tot.

In the land of thoughts, I'm a tourist lost,
With a ticket to nowhere, at what cost?
They laugh and giggle, these whimsical chums,
As I ponder the meaning of spaghetti and crumbs.

Whispers of Fleeting Thoughts

I had a plan, don't ask me when,
It slipped away like a mischievous friend.
With coffee and dreams, I lined them up tight,
But now I can't recall, was it wrong or right?

Balloons in the sky, or was it my brain?
Chasing the echoes, it's all just a game.
I scribble my notes, in a paper boat,
Sailing the rivers of thoughts that don't float.

Chasing Shadows in the Mind

I tried to catch thoughts, like bubbles in air,
But they pop with a giggle, 'Oh, do you care?'
I chased the bright ideas, oh such a sight,
Only to find them in the fridge tonight.

One minute I'm wise, the next I'm a fool,
With the wisdom of squirrels that live in the pool.
My thoughts are like socks, on a laundry spree,
Always missing in action, where can they be?

A Dance of Forgotten Intentions

I set my ambitions to dance in a row,
In a box marked 'someday', they put on a show.
But what was the tune? I forgot the refrain,
Now they tango with chaos and laugh at my pain.

With breakfast ideas that turn into toast,
I ponder what matters, but smile at the most.
Intentions like jelly, they wiggle and slide,
Gathering dust, letting whims be my guide.

Ephemeral Questions

Why did I enter this room with a grin?
Was it to ponder the meaning of sin?
Or maybe a snack is what I was after,
Unlocking the mystery with laughter and rapture.

The answers, they dance like fireflies bright,
Flickering visions that dart out of sight.
I chuckle and shout, 'What was my point?'
As the universe giggles, my thoughts are disjoint.

Silence in the Midst of Chaos

In a room full of chatter, I blankly stare,
Thoughts swirling around like they don't even care.
Did I leave the oven on or was it my phone?
Ah, the chaos sings sweetly, I'm never alone.

Amidst kids running wild and dishes that stack,
I ponder my purpose or what I might lack.
Maybe it's chocolate or dancing in rain,
In this whirlwind of madness, I embrace the insane.

The Puzzle of Perplexing Thoughts

With pieces that scatter, I search for the edge,
Each thought a new color, each moment a pledge.
Did I step on my cat or open a door?
I giggle and wonder, who's keeping the score?

Conundrums and riddles that twist in my brain,
Like socks that go missing, they drive me insane.
Yet laughter erupts like a bubbling stream,
Revealing the nonsense within every dream.

Reflections in a Broken Mirror

I glance at my image, a quirky dismay,
Who's that smiling madly in such a weird way?
A wink and a grimace, confusion runs wild,
Life's little antics—who needs to be mild?

Cracks in the glass show my silly affairs,
Like half-finished puzzles and mismatched pairs.
With humor the lens, I'll see clear today,
In this jumbled reflection, I'm happy to play.

Between the Lines of Laughter

In the margins of jokes, wisdom hides well,
Wrapped tight in the punchlines, a trickster's spell.
With giggles as fuel, we dash through the jest,
Chasing the moments that feel like the best.

So here in the gray, with a wink and a smile,
I ponder my journey, if just for a while.
Life's laughter is fleeting, a whirlwind of cheer,
And now, what was I saying? Oh, never you fear!

When Curiosity Fades

Once I had questions galore,
Now I just laugh and implore.
Thoughts slip away like a breeze,
What was I saying? Oh please!

Days often blend into night,
Errors become quite a sight.
Wonders dissolve like a mist,
Oh look! I made a new twist.

Pondering deep, I would dive,
But soon, my brain took a drive.
Ideas flutter off to play,
Hey! Wait, what was I today?

Now I just giggle and smile,
Forget what confused me a while.
Curiosity's a great game,
But now, I can't even name.

The Art of Forgetting

Memory's a slippery fish,
Caught in a net of my wish.
What was the plan? Was it fun?
Maybe I'll know by next run.

Notes piled high, they all blur,
Things I once thought to confer.
The mind's a maze, quite absurd,
Wait, did I just hear a bird?

Alas, I thought I was wise,
Trapped in the web of my sighs.
Yet here I chuckle and gloat,
Did I forget? Or just float?

The art of forgetting's okay,
Brightens my silly old day.
I laugh at the things I won't keep,
Funny how thoughts just can leap.

Whims of an Uncertain Heart

A flutter here, a giggle there,
My heart is dancing without a care.
What was my goal? Can't recall,
Let's just enjoy this free-for-all.

Plans once firm, now a haze,
I'm lost in this intricate daze.
Never thought I'd drift this way,
But who even knows? Hooray!

Romantic ideas take flight,
Each whim just feels so right.
Caught up in a whimsicle chase,
What's my name? Lift off with grace.

Though paths may twist, they unfold,
Uncertain hearts are fun to behold.
Forget what I meant, let it part,
In laughter, we find our true art.

The Intricacies of an Unasked Question

A thought lingers, oh so shy,
It flutters past, then says goodbye.
I ponder deeply, but who cares?
Did I even need to prepare?

Questions roam like playful thought,
Answers tangled, easily caught.
Wait, did I want to disclose?
Or is this just how life flows?

An inquiry lost in the fray,
Just floating on, come what may.
Chasing whispers of a chat,
Excuse me, what was I at?

Still, it's fun to be in the mist,
For answers always seem to twist.
Forget the ask, let laughter shine,
What's a question? Oh, that's divine!

The Flick of a Distant Star

A glimmer lights the sky tonight,
I wonder if it's quite the sight.
Did I leave my coffee on the stove?
Oh shoot! I'm lost in thought, I rove.

The cosmos winks, I squint and stare,
What's that twinkling? Who knows or cares?
Maybe I should just focus here,
But my mind flies far, without a steer.

Juggling thoughts like clumsy stars,
Do I need sleep? Or coffee bars?
This universe, a joke on pause,
I laugh so hard, it gives no cause.

With laughter echoing in the void,
I ponder why I'm so annoyed.
Wait, did I really lose my train?
Let's dance on clouds and laugh in rain!

Threads of Thought in a Cosmic Weave

A thread gets tangled in my mind,
What was I saying? Never mind!
The universe spins, I start to grin,
As I trip on thoughts and fall within.

Each notion zigzags, goes astray,
I swear I had a point today.
But then a squirrel distracts my gaze,
Oh look! A shiny thing that plays!

Life feels like a silly game of chess,
Oh wait, was that a crucial guess?
A cosmic laugh, or just my fate?
I'll have some fries while I wait.

So let the stars align their jokes,
I'll chase my tail while time provokes.
Let's dance with thoughts like cosmic dust,
Who needs a plan? Oh, it's a must!

Mindscapes of a Restless Dreamer

In dreams, I sail on clouds of cream,
Where thoughts collide, and laughter beams.
A reason floats, then bounces back,
Hold on! I'm train-spotting, oh, what lack!

I scribble notes on napkins wide,
To capture wisdom I can't decide.
Oh wait, was I supposed to write?
I should just nap; that feels just right.

Between a chuckle and a sigh,
Life's a riddle, oh my, oh my!
I'll dive through puddles, splash about,
And leave 'em guessing, filled with doubt.

Yet here I am, a restless soul,
Trying to play a vital role.
But if I trip and land in glee,
Let's toast to life's absurdity!

The Illusion of Intent versus Reality

Thoughts like bubbles floating high,
Pop! And then I wave goodbye.
Was I meant to focus here?
Or did I lose my mind, oh dear!

Intentions often clash and slide,
Like socks that vanish when we glide.
Reality laughs, a cheeky sprite,
Who needs a map when lost feels right?

With every step, I trip and fall,
But laughter rises over it all.
"Why was I here?" I scratch my head,
Oh look! A donut! Let's be fed!

So dance, dear friends, and let it go,
This crazy ride's the greatest show.
Intentions may twist like a kite,
But let's keep soaring, feeling light!

Laughter in the Depths of Confusion

In a world of endless chatter,
Thoughts wander like a lost sheep.
I start to spill my wisdom,
But oops, now I'm half asleep.

The coffee's cold, the socks don't match,
I laugh as logic takes a break.
Why do I wander in my thoughts?
Oh look, a butterfly, for goodness' sake!

With every step, I trip on air,
And joke about my scattered brain.
If only I could find my keys,
But wait, I forgot what I just gained!

So here's to laughs in the confusion,
Where senses seem to lose their place.
I raise a toast to missing thoughts,
And dance around in endless space.

Moments Lost In a Daydream

Dreaming while I wash the dishes,
My mind takes flight, oh what a scene!
I've built a castle in the clouds,
But where's my fork? It's left unseen.

A squirrel starts a heated debate,
About the best way to climb a tree.
I nod, yet lose my grip on time,
Time for lunch? Or was it tea?

Each thought a butterfly in flight,
I chase them down like they're a prize.
They flit away just out of reach,
And giggles form behind my eyes.

Was I talking to the laundry?
Or did I order pizza too?
In this daydream state of mine,
Life's a circus, fun and askew.

Reflections on a Dusty Path

Wandering down a winding road,
I ponder if I've lost my way.
A sign says left, but my shoes squeak,
And I'm not sure if I should stay.

The trees gossip to each other,
While the sun winks, oh what a tease.
I stop to pet a passing cloud,
And wonder if it knows my cheese.

Thoughts tumble like the autumn leaves,
What was my question, where's the map?
I hear a laugh from deep inside,
As I trip over a friendly sap.

But dust is good, it sticks around,
And so does laughter in the breeze.
I'll just meander on this path,
Embracing questions with such ease.

Questions in the Silence

In the stillness, thoughts collide,
Like cats who're napping in the sun.
What was I doing? Was it lunch?
Oh look, my shoelace came undone.

The echo of my absent mind,
Makes all my worries seem so light.
Did I forget to feed the fish?
Or did I train them to take flight?

I ponder deep and then I laugh,
At life's peculiar, twisty turns.
With every question, joy is found,
As curiosity still burns.

In silence, wonders start to bloom,
And laughter dances in the air.
If answers hide, I won't despair,
I'll make a joke, without a care.

Captured in the Stillness of Distraction

In the corner, a sock sits alone,
Forgotten thoughts on a phone.
Coffee's gone cold, my toast burnt,
What was I doing? Oh, it's adjourned.

Popsicles melting in summer's heat,
Just like my brain, feels like defeat.
I search for the keys, but they're not there,
Chasing dreams, but wait—what's for dinner wear?

The cat's done a dance, while I sip tea,
What was this all about? Was it just me?
The clock ticks on, but I'm stuck in place,
Notes in my head, oh, what a silly chase!

The light flickers once, then twice, maybe thrice,
Thoughts drift away, like a shoe with a slice.
Was it a plan, a workshop tonight?
Or just a delightful stroll in my own mind's fight?

The Drift of Time and Memory

Time slips away, like ice cream in sun,
Hold on a second—now, what's my fun?
A thought pops up, then flutters away,
Right after I think, "Hey, what was my day?"

In a daze, I ponder the meaning of toast,
Yet here I am, wanting the crispy most.
My cats hatch plots, they watch me stare,
Did I need that grocery list? Oh, where's my pair?

Maybe it's fate, or just silly chance,
Each day's a comedy, a laughable dance.
A wanderer's path with no clear design,
Why was I here? Oh, was it wine time?

Under bright skies, confusion's a friend,
One moment of clarity, then back on the mend.
The sun's going down, should I chase it away?
Wait, what was I doing? Oh, just another day.

The Silent Symphony of Unsung Moments

A symphony plays in the back of my mind,
But the conductor's lost—ah, what did I find?
Balloons are floating, as thoughts intertwine,
What was I saying? Oh, but that's fine!

Laughter erupts from a sneeze at the table,
Is this a meeting, or just am I able?
Baking a cake, I forgot the main plan,
And suddenly realized—who put me in charge, man?

Chasing my thoughts down each winding road,
Like running in circles, but never unload.
The blender's whirring, it drowns out my song,
What was that thing? Oh, where did I go wrong?

Bubbles in soda, like time drifting past,
The clock keeps on ticking, moves way too fast.
It's fine to be lost, in fact, it's a game,
What was I saying? Perhaps I forgot your name!

The Spectrum of Fleeting Awareness

A laugh escapes on the way to the fridge,
Forgotten thoughts flutter like a little midge.
I ponder life's meaning, or was it my shoes?
Oh wait, is that cookie still there to peruse?

A cat just yawned, did I mention it's cute?
Suddenly my worries dissolve like old fruit.
I think about dinner, or maybe nap time,
Whispers of wisdom, but all sound like mime.

I once had a goal, it was really profound,
But now it's lost somewhere, not to be found.
Reflections remain as I chase after flies,
Maybe tomorrow, or not, where's my fries?

The clock keeps on ticking, yet who keeps the score?
With thoughts like these, I could barely wish more.
I might be a sage, but it's hard to be sure,
Especially when snacks make my heart feel secure.

Reflections on a Forgetful Breeze

I once had a plan, it was drawn on a napkin,
But now it just flutters like a bird, could it happen?
Thoughts come and go like the wind through the trees,
What was I doing? Ah, just to please my knees.

A butterfly lands, its colors all bright,
And suddenly questions take off in flight.
What was my point? Was it something profound?
Or did I just want to be out on the ground?

My coffee's grown cold, much like my intent,
But that's just fine, 'cause I'm quite content.
Life's swirling around like a dance on a dime,
As I laugh with the leaves, forgetting the rhyme.

So here I stand, in meandering thought,
With a chuckle at fate, and a mind that's just fraught.
Maybe tomorrow will bring something new,
For now, let's just see what the squirrels will do.

The Weight of Watercolor Dreams

Brush strokes of memories run wild in my mind,
Each hue telling stories, though none are aligned.
I paint with my thoughts, oh what a delight,
Yet every new color feels like a lost fight.

Was that a great banquet, or just Tuesday's meal?
Dreams drip like watercolor, with a whimsical feel.
I carry my canvas, though unsure of the scene,
Maybe it's breakfast, or just some ice cream?

With every brush flick, new wonders awaken,
I'm blending the moments, though some I have taken.
What was I saying whilst mixing the shades?
Oh look, there's a giraffe in my lemonade!

Each stroke a reminder of chaos and cheer,
Yet all I can think of is what's for next year.
Life's a canvas stretched thin, much like my resolve,
With each sip of confusion, new colors dissolve.

Questions Slide Into the Abyss

Inquiry dances, prances, plays at my door,
Each question a jig, yet one I ignore.
What was the question? Oh, maybe the snack!
Where'd I leave my keys? Oh, they must be back.

Mind like a fish, darting under bright beams,
Chasing elusive thoughts, or perhaps just sweet creams.
Is it too early for a nap or a third?
The abyss offers laughter, where all dreams are stirred.

I ponder existence while stuck in a chair,
Was that profound, or just a light glare?
What did I need? Oh, it's slipping away,
Just like my change, beneath couch pillows sway.

So here I will linger, a smile on my lips,
In the swirling unknown, with all of life's quips.
Tomorrow will come with its own set of views,
But today, I'll just munch on some blissful Chews.

The Maze of Existence

In this puzzling haze I dwell,
Each fork and twist, a tale to tell.
I start to ponder, then I pause,
What was the question? Oh, just because.

I chase a thought, it's gone like mist,
Right when I think it can't be missed.
A rabbit hole, a sly delight,
I'll just follow—wait, it's night!

With every turn, a fresh surprise,
A dance of quirks behind my eyes.
When did I start? Oh, no idea,
But it's much better with pizza here!

So round and round I gladly roam,
Wandering lost yet feeling home.
A laugh, a smile, as I embrace,
The funny moments in this chase.

When Silences Speak

In awkward pauses, words collide,
The chuckles rise, we can't decide.
Expressions funny, oh what a mess,
Did I forget? Or just digress?

A nod, a smile, then nothing more,
What was it now? An open door.
Silences blast, like confetti flies,
Each giggle whispers, just say bye!

I'll sip my tea, and ponder hard,
Those vacant spaces, they're not marred.
Inside my head, the ruckus plays,
What's next? I'm stuck in this daze.

But oh, these giggles bring me light,
In silly moments, all feels right.
I sip, I laugh, the moments blend,
And guess what? I can't comprehend!

Echoes of Unfinished Sentences

I started speaking, lost my track,
The echoes linger, feeling whack.
Did I really mean to say that line?
Or was I craving pizza and wine?

Words tumble out, then fade away,
Right before they could have their say.
The punchline waits, I'm left in shock,
A thought to share? But now it's locked.

Questions linger, I jest and grin,
While perfect answers hide within.
I reach to catch what comes alive,
But all I have is a funny jive.

The silence fills the room with grace,
As laughter paints a silly face.
In all this fluff, I find delight,
My half-spoken truth, a merry sight.

Wandering Through Uncertainty

Where am I going, oh what a maze,
Each step I take, it shifts and sways.
I feel like dancing, but wait, my shoe?
Ah well, I'll prance in mismatched too!

A world of questions, I prance along,
With silly tunes, I sing my song.
What's left behind? A fractured thought,
Yet in this dance, confusion's caught.

With giggles floating through the air,
I juggle dreams, just like a bear.
The path's unclear, but so much fun,
Is that a cloud or just my run?

Embrace the wander, let it flow,
With a twinkle in my eye, I go.
With laughter bright, I skip around,
In this sweet chaos, joy is found.

The Art of Losing Focus

In a room filled with chatter, I sit and I stare,
Searching for wonders that float in the air.
A sip of my drink, and the thought goes away,
What was I doing? I'll figure it the next day.

I glance at my phone; it dings every hour,
Was I supposed to remember some great power?
The cat on the window, so fluffy and wide,
Says, 'Chase me instead; there's no need to decide!'

The clock on the wall plays a game of its own,
Reminding me gently, I'm not all alone.
My list of great plans lies forgotten and lost,
Oh look, there's that sandwich: delicious, but frost!

I laugh at the notion of grand goals and schemes,
When laughter and giggles are better than dreams.
For life's just a game, with puzzles galore,
And sometimes forgetting is worth so much more!

In Search of Elusive Truths

With maps in my head, I'm on a grand quest,
To find hidden truths, but they never seem best.
A squirrel jogs by, looking wise and refined,
I ask it for answers, but it's busy, never mind!

I ponder the stars, how they twinkle at night,
Yet pondering leaves me more tangled than bright.
A thought in my brain is like fire on ice,
Just when I hold it, it vanishes—how nice!

The grass whispers secrets, but I can't comprehend,
Like chasing a mirage that calls like a friend.
A riddle so puzzling, yet beautifully clear,
If I don't stop searching, what will I hear?

Yet maybe it's fine to just let go and play,
Embrace all the nonsense that comes on the way.
For truths are like bubbles: they pop in the wind,
And laughter's the joy that the silence rescinds.

Thoughts Like Clouds at Dusk

Thoughts float like clouds as the evening sets in,
Drifting on breezes where few have been.
One moment I'm wise, then I trip on my shoe,
Did I need that wisdom, or was I just due?

A deep thought arrives, like a gust in the night,
Then poof! It is gone, like a deer in quick flight.
I question my questions—are they real or a jest?
Maybe walking in circles is simply the best.

The sun sets low, painting stories in gold,
Yet my mind is like taffy; it stretches, then folds.
A giggle escapes, as I shake off the trance,
Sometimes it's all silly, a whimsical dance.

And so, as I ponder these clouds overhead,
I laugh at my journey, no reason for dread.
For life spins like cosmos, both wild and serene,
And every lost thought is a new adventure unseen!

When Questions Dance in Silence

In quiet moments, questions pirouette,
Whirling and twirling, what will come next?
A slip of my mind, like a tiptoe on ice,
What was I asking? Could someone think twice?

Do fish ponder rivers, or cats their own tails?
What do we find in the world of our trails?
Amidst all these wonders, I lose my own path,
Chasing down shadows that giggle with wrath.

If answers were candy, would I get a spree?
But searching for candy is tough, don't you see?
So I chuckle at queries that leap out of bounds,
Pretending I'm wise while reality confounds.

Each question a puzzle, each silence a game,
And I'm just the jester, though I'm never the same.
Embracing the chaos, I twirl in delight,
For even in questions, there's laughter at night.

The Paradox of Living

Each morning I wake, coffee in hand,
Contemplating choices, both silly and grand.
Yet thoughts fly away like a kite in the breeze,
I remind myself gently, 'Oh, do as you please.'

With socks on my hands, I'm prepared for the day,
And ponder the meaning, then lose it mid-way.
Life feels like a dance, two steps to the left,
But all of my partners seem utterly bereft.

I scribble down notes on a napkin of fate,
Of wisdom and insight—the pages equate.
But when I read back, it's all quite absurd,
Like trying to catch every fifth flying bird.

So here's to the chaos, let laughter ignite,
For missing the point seems a comical plight.
I'll chuckle through life's not-so-ordered course,
And enjoy the absurd as a fanciful force.

Fragments of a Fading Memory

I woke up this morning, aware of the scheme,
Yet suddenly found I had lost all my steam.
Where did the laughter from yesterday go?
Oh wait, was it breakfast? I really don't know!

I tried to recall what I wanted to do,
But all that I found was a sock in my shoe.
The cat gave me looks, as if to suggest,
That chasing my brain is a humorous quest.

The errands I planned slipped away in a blur,
My thoughts like lost sneakers, in search of a fur.
At lunchtime I pondered what I should next grab,
But only my tupperware gave me the jab.

So here's to the moments of fleeting delight,
When laughter escapes in the dead of the night.
For life's little puzzles are best shared with cheer,
As fragments of memory dance ever near.

Footprints In a Clouded Mind

I stepped on a cloud with my head in the air,
Thought I saw wisdom, then it vanished—oh where?
The ground underneath seemed to giggle and squirm,
While I tried to tether each playful term.

With lists I would write, and my pen was on fire,
But mixed in a jiffy—what's next? I retire!
A phrase on the tip of my tongue, so divine,
Yet poof! it eludes, oh how fleeting's the line!

I wander through thoughts like a child on a spree,
While questions and answers play hide-and-go-seek.
Was it a dream, or a joke from the past?
With giggles of fate, I make moments last.

So let's laugh at the trails we leave in the mist,
For clarity muddles in a dance we can't resist.
In clouds we may stumble, but joy's ever near,
With footprints of laughter, let's cheer without fear.

Tracing the Lines of Existence

I doodle on napkins, a map of the great,
But scribbles turn heads to a wobbly fate.
Connections I'm making are rarely in place,
As lines twist and bend in a whimsical chase.

Searching for meaning in the tea leaves I brew,
I spilled half the cup—oh, what could I do?
Like tracing the stars that refuse to stay still,
I grasp at the wonders, yet dream of a mill.

A conversation starts, but the punchline's a fog,
As laughter escapes like a run-away dog.
Yet here lies the fun, in the mix-up we find,
In tracing our paths with a curious mind.

So let's celebrate chaos, the joy of the game,
Where purpose will tickle and hide just the same.
For existence is wobbly, a curious ride,
With laughter our compass, we'll wander with pride.

Whispers of a Wandering Mind

I ponder deep, then drift away,
What was I thinking, anyway?
A thought like butterflies on a spree,
Dancing wildly, just like me.

A squirrel darts past, with a nut in tow,
I laugh and forget the deep, wise flow.
Maybe it's coffee, or too much snack,
Whatever it is, I can't get it back.

A puzzle piece lost in endless tide,
I chase my thoughts, like they're on a slide.
They giggle and tumble, like kids at play,
Where was I going? Oh, look! A stray.

In the chaos of giggles and fun,
I grasp at understanding, but it's gone.
Is wisdom a whisper? A joke on repeat?
I'll laugh it off, and dance on my feet.

Footprints on a Shifting Path

Steps I take, they twist and bend,
Am I lost? Or just pretend?
Each footprint fades in shifting sand,
Wait, what was I trying to plan?

I chase a thought and trip on air,
Falling down without a care.
A path appears, then vanishes wide,
Like socks in laundry, they all collide.

A voice in my head, it sings a song,
But melody's lost; oh where did it belong?
I sway and twirl, lost in this dance,
What was my point? I can't take the chance.

With laughter ringing and giggles aflame,
Perhaps it's silly? Or just a game?
Footprints lead nowhere, but that's okay,
Let's just enjoy this wandering play.

Flickers of Clarity in Confusion

Bright sparks of thought, oh how they gleam,
Then they flutter off, like a wild dream.
I scratch my head, where did they go?
Was it a thought, or just a show?

A joke slips out, but who's to know?
Laughter is gold; let it overflow!
A flicker of brilliance sets my heart free,
But wait, what was it? Let it be me.

I wander through mazes of crazy ideas,
Tripping on laughter, drowning in cheers.
What was the thought? It's a merry-go-round,
Yet joy finds a way to stick around.

When clarity whispers, it teases my mind,
A fleeting moment, oh so kind.
I shake off the fog, let happiness spin,
What was I after? Oh, let's just begin!

Moments Unraveled in Time

Tick-tock echoes and time slips by,
I glance at the clock and wonder why.
Moments unravel, like threads from a seam,
Wait, was I there? Or lost in a dream?

A cup of tea, a cookie or two,
I munch my thoughts, oh what to do?
In the deep end, I swim with a grin,
But where was I headed? Lost in a spin.

Jokes hang like stars, twinkling with glee,
Each giggle a spark, setting me free.
Was it all real? Or playfully shy?
Moments blend in a pie in the sky.

So let's celebrate laughter and jest,
With moments unwrapped, we'll do our best.
Though life may confuse and twist like a rhyme,
Let's frolic together, lose sense of time.

The Fable of Forgotten Awareness

Once a wise owl sat in a tree,
He pondered so hard, he forgot his tea.
With thoughts all tangled, a curious spree,
He muttered aloud, "What was that? Oh me!"

A squirrel scurried, cheeky and spry,
"Did you lose something, friend? You seem awry!"
The owl just blinked, with a puzzled sigh,
"I was thinking of... oh wait, I can't try!"

In circles they danced, round and round,
Searching for meaning, but none could be found.
The grass whispered secrets, the sun bounced around,
But clarity vanished, like echoes unbound!

So they laughed at the chase of thoughts unclear,
Chasing their tails, shedding a tear.
"Life's a wild ride," the owl said with cheer,
"Let's sip on this joy, never fear, my dear!"

Ink Splotches of Understanding

A writer once penned with much flair,
Yet spilled ink everywhere without a care.
"What was I saying?" he pulled at his hair,
As his words dripped on paper, a colorful affair.

With splashes of blue, and streaks of green,
His thoughts turned into a messy cuisine.
Each sentence a puzzle, none quite seen,
He chuckled, "These splotches are truly obscene!"

A cat on the desk licked the ink,
With a swish of its tail, it dared to think.
"I'm pretty sure, if you'll let me wink,
That all your musings are lost in a blink!"

So the writer just laughed, abandoned the fight,
"Life's a grand jester, it's all kind of light.
With every ink splotch, wrong feels so right,
Let's scribble our joy, let's embrace the night!"

Recollecting Fragments of Time

In a cupboard of thoughts, I stashed my dreams,
But every now and then, they burst at the seams.
I'd chase after memories, or so it seems,
Only to find they're lost in the beams!

A clock ticked loudly, "What's your grand plan?"
I shrugged and said, "If only I ran...
Wait, wait! Was I meant to engage in a ban?"
But I stubbed my toe, and that was the span.

Soup simmering slowly, on the back of the stove,
I pondered life's meaning while playing with a grove.
"Is it in laughter, in love, in the trove?"
But the question got lost, like a sincere cove.

So I twirled in the kitchen, forgot what I sought,
Blending adventure with all that I bought.
My life's a fragmented, whimsical plot,
Each piece a reminder, though often forgot!

When the Mind Takes Flight and Falters

An eagle soared high, thoughts in the air,
But mid-flight, it stumbled, lost in despair.
"What was my mission?" it gasped, unaware,
As clouds giggled softly, showing their flair.

Its wings started flapping in odd little twirls,
An awkward dance amongst daisies and pearls.
The skies erupted with fits of warm swirls,
The eagle then pondered, "Does life have swirls?"

A chatty parrot landed, bright as a jam,
"Hey buddy, slow down! You're looking quite cram!
Just chill with the breeze, take a look at the glam,
Life's not a race, it's a whimsical slam!"

The eagle then chuckled, shaking off woe,
And glided down gently, enjoying the flow.
"Perhaps I forgot, why rush? Why not go,
With laughter and joy in this lovely tableau?"

Beyond the Veil of Reason

In shadows where thoughts entwine,
I ponder if coffee's divine.
Yet, amidst all this grand analysis,
Did I leave the stove on? What a mess!

With logic tied in knots, I muse,
Should I wear those bright pink shoes?
A cat on the floor, it's quite the scene,
Did I forget to check my routine?

Glimpses of wisdom dance and swirl,
Like socks that vanish in a whirl.
Did I just drop my train of thought?
Or was it just a clever plot?

So here I sit, with joy and zest,
In this chaotic, quirky quest.
Embracing nonsense, light and free,
Like leaves that twirl on a whimsy spree.

The Hazy Road Less Traveled

I walk a path that twists and bends,
With thoughts that start but never end.
A squirrel darts by, caught in the chase,
Was there something I needed to face?

With breadcrumbs leading to nowhere fast,
I muse on moments, memories cast.
Lost in laughter, I trip and roll,
Wait, what was my original goal?

A turtle is crossing; I pause with glee,
Is it wise to follow or just let it be?
A map in my pocket, upside down,
I think I'm lost in this merry town.

Each turn brings a giggle, a moment of fun,
Chasing thoughts like elusive sun.
On this road, I find joy in the ride,
As I stumble through life, eyes open wide.

Navigating the Spiral of Thoughts

Round and round, my thoughts do spin,
Did I really mean to venture in?
Like a washing machine on a spree,
Dizzy wondering if I have to pee.

In whirlwinds of wonder, I chase a clue,
What was that thing I meant to do?
With each twist, there's giggles and sighs,
Perhaps I should keep a list by my fries.

A duck quacks loudly, longing to play,
And I'm reminded, it's just one of those days.
Oh, tasks and duties, where did you go?
Life's just a game, with laughs in tow.

I give my brain a playful shove,
Caught in the web of warm fuzzy love.
As the spiral whirls me up and around,
I find my laughter where joy must be found.

Streams of Consciousness in Motion

Oh look! A cloud that looks like cheese,
How did I end up pondering these?
The puddles reflect a kaleidoscope bright,
Where did I hide my plans for tonight?

Each thought is a rabbit, I chase with glee,
Was I meant to follow or just let it be?
A parade of wonders, both silly and spry,
Is that my name they just called from the sky?

The socks in my drawer are plotting a scheme,
In a world made of marshmallows, oh what a dream!
And wait, what was it that I had to do?
A map of nonsense, to guide me anew.

In streams that bubble and giggle and flow,
I twirl through the chaos, just going with the flow.
With laughter as my compass, I find sweet delight,
In the blur of existence, I embrace the light.

Navigating the Unknown

In an ocean of thoughts, I float,
Chasing dreams on a leaky boat.
Maps that I draw seem all askew,
But hey, I'll figure it out—maybe two.

Clouds of confusion gather and part,
Can't remember why it all must start.
Navigating shores of 'what could be',
But oops! Did I just spill my tea?

With every turn, a new surprise,
Like stepping outside in mismatched ties.
The compass spins, the hourglass melts,
Guess I'll roll with whatever life feels.

So here's to finding my own strange way,
With giggles and guffaws leading the play.
I'll wander far, but I'll be alright—
As long as there's ice cream in sight.

What Lies Beneath the Surface

Underneath the serious facade,
A jester dances, oh so far from the charade.
Truths that bubble beneath the skin,
Like when you laugh before the joke can begin.

I dive deep into thoughts so profound,
Where fish wear glasses and cats serenade sound.
What lies beneath? Oh, the giggling spores,
Where logic takes breaks and nonsense explores.

Fish with umbrellas sail in the stream,
They question my wisdom—'What's your grand scheme?'

Perhaps it's just laughter, a quirky delight,
That makes all the chaos feel perfectly right.

So let's lift the curtain and have a good look,
At sparkly nonsense, the world's little nook.
What's beneath? Just a glorious mess,
And maybe a cupcake—life's sweetest finesse.

Caught Between Purpose and Distraction

With purpose in one hand and snacks in the other,
I ponder life's meaning with my favorite mother.
But whispers of Netflix call out my name,
Competing for focus—oh, what a game!

Should I march forward with plans and resolve?
Or scroll through my feed—an eternal dissolve?
Caught in the middle of 'should''s and 'must''s,
Like a squirrel deciding which nut to trust.

Between joy and duty, I sway like a tree,
Branches of laughter tickle my knee.
What road to take? The question is key,
But first, let me check what's on TV.

In the end, it's a balancing act,
Of binge watching wisdom woven with fact.
So here's to the jolt of distractions, my friend,
Where purpose is fleeting, but giggles won't end.

A Symphony of Half-Known Truths

In a symphony hall where questions collide,
A kazoo plays softly, confusion our guide.
Strings pluck the logic, but brass steals the show,
As melodies mingle in a topsy-turvy flow.

The conductor, well-meaning, waves a nice wand,
But the flutes are striking up random grandstands.
A half-known truth—what does it mean?
Maybe it swirls in a tango scoff scene.

With ducks in bowties performing a jig,
And popcorn falling down with every gig.
Each note a reminder of wondering why,
Life's circus unfolds as the tunes drift by.

So sway with the rhythm, let laughter compose,
Even when meaning eludes like a rose.
In this zany symphony, take a great leap,
For half-known truths are the secrets we keep.

The Tapestry of Tangential Tales

In a bustling café, I sip my tea,
Memories flit by, but where could they be?
A squirrel steals the spotlight, running in haste,
Reminding me of dreams I often chased.

Conversations swirl like leaves in the breeze,
"Did I forget lunch? Or just my keys?"
A cat on the counter, judging so sly,
Whispers of wisdom, but why, oh why?

Riddles wrapped in laughter, jests intertwined,
A movie plays softly, but what's on my mind?
The punchline escapes without even a trace,
Yet joy is a journey, not just a race.

With each twist and turn, I'm lost, then I find,
The thrill of confusion is awfully kind.
For in this circus, that life can be,
It's perfectly fine just to be, you see.

Clarity Amidst the Clutter

A messy desk holds treasures yet unmet,
Papers like clouds, where thoughts can forget.
Coffee cups stack in a precarious tower,
Was I waiting for genius or just the next hour?

Fuzzy memories dance on the edge of my brain,
Like trying to recall a forgotten refrain.
A not-so-great idea becomes a great joke,
Amidst all the chaos, I laugh 'til I choke.

Notifications ping, but I'm lost in a task,
What was the question? Oh, dare I ask?
The clutter surrounds me, yet brings me delight,
In this comedic maze, the future's so bright.

Every lost thought feels like part of the play,
As life rolls along in a curious way.
In chaos exists a whimsical grace,
Each confusion brings smiles to the face.

In Pursuit of Fleeting Wisdom

Chasing down gnomes with a map made of dreams,
I ponder on knowledge, or so it seems.
A wise old owl gives a look of dismay,
Maybe I'm lost — should I head the other way?

Between bites of pizza, pondering deep,
Discoveries bubble, then suddenly leap.
A fortune cookie hints with a cryptic grin,
But I can't quite remember where I've been.

Nonsense spills forth like a river in flood,
The quest for the answer feels more like a thud.
Yet laughter erupts with every odd choice,
Which rings louder now? The chaos or voice?

But wisdom, I find, is a playful disguise,
In the act of forgetting, we sharpen our eyes.
So if you trip over a thought or a shoe,
Just giggle and dance; it's just what we do.

Ephemeral Glimpses of Clarity

In flashes of brilliance, my mind hits a spark,
Yet within a heartbeat, it fades into dark.
Questions like fireflies flit in the night,
I chase after thoughts just to get them in sight.

Sticky post-its cover my wall like a quilt,
Each scribble and doodle—a tapestry built.
A sudden thought bubbles, but then it departs,
Leaving only echoes of half-drawn charts.

The quest for the answer feels like an illusion,
A wild goose chase in a joyful confusion.
But finding a laugh in the midst of the mess,
Brings forth a warmth; I couldn't care less.

So here in this chaos, with whimsy in hand,
I dance through the questions, as life's giggles stand.
For even amid muddles, clarity gleams,
As laughter reminds me to follow my dreams.

A Journey Through Fleeting Moments

In a race with time, I dash,
Chasing thoughts that come and clash.
Oh look, a squirrel! It paused my grind,
Now where's that thought? I'm in a bind.

Life's like a donut, sweet and round,
But glaze gets sticky, wonder is found.
I had a point, it slipped away,
Just like my socks on laundry day.

The clock is ticking, oh so loud,
Yet here I stand, feeling quite proud.
Wait, was I doing something grand?
Or just daydreaming in a wonderland?

Each moment's fleeting, like candy floss,
Deliciously sweet, but where's the gloss?
I'll jot it down, then lose the pen,
So now I'm back to wondering when.

The Subtle Science of Distraction

Oh look, a butterfly, bright and bold,
But what was that fact I was told?
Distractions dance like stars at night,
Each twirl makes my brain take flight.

I sip my tea, forget the brew,
Did my toast burn? Oh, who knew!
My mind's a circus, clowns and all,
Yet I still forget what I call.

The brain's a puzzle, pieces stray,
Like socks in the dryer, gone to play.
I had a notion, it was profound,
Now it's lost, nowhere to be found.

What was I saying? Oh right, the game,
No, wait, it slipped, what was the name?
Chasing thoughts like bubbles in air,
Pop! There goes another, do I care?

Unraveling the Threads of Existence

Life's like knitting, threads all askew,
I dropped a stitch, who knew it grew?
The fabric of thoughts, tangled so tight,
Now my scarf looks more like a kite!

In every moment, a laugh, a sigh,
Wait, did I just tell the same lie?
My stories twirl like spaghetti sauce,
Now everything's lost, oh what a toss!

In the tapestry of dreams I weave,
Lost in a thought no one can believe.
I had a goal, it slipped my mind,
Is it in this sock, or left behind?

Life's a riddle, a game of charades,
I scratch my head, all thoughts evade.
Where was the punchline, the funny twist?
Oh wait, I just lost it in the mist.

Fading Echoes of Intention

Echoes whisper like shadows on wall,
What was the question? I can't recall.
Thoughts flutter by, like leaves in the breeze,
Caught in a whirlwind, oh if you please!

I thought I had wisdom, wrapped in a bow,
But then I tripped on the way to show.
The more I say, the less it connects,
It's like playing charades with all the wrong specs.

I scribble down notes on crumpled up paper,
But now they look like a cryptic caper.
Intention's a ghost, it chuckles and fades,
Leaving me puzzled, caught in cascades.

So here I sit, in a whimsical dance,
Thinking of thoughts that lost their chance.
What was the point? Oh dear, what a fuss,
Just pass me a donut, and let's make a fuss!

Dancing With Distraction

In a world where thoughts collide,
I juggle tasks, oh what a ride.
Coffee cup in hand, I trip and spill,
Awake or dreaming? The lines are thin.

Chasing whims like butterflies,
While to-do lists grow, oh how they rise!
Laughter echoes amidst the haze,
Am I lost, or just in a daze?

A text ping sparks an urge to roam,
From dish to dance, I call it home.
The clock ticks on, yet here I sway,
Tomorrow's chores can wait, hooray!

So let's embrace this merry game,
Distraction's charm is never lame.
With every step, I find my groove,
In the whirl, I learn to move.

The Soundtrack of a Silent Storm

Thoughts whistle softly like a breeze,
Words escape me, like leaves from trees.
I nod along to tunes in my head,
But can't recall what was just said.

An owl hoots a soothing tune,
While I search for words, higher than the moon.
Lost in rhythm, I sway and hum,
Words dance away, where did they run?

A riddle wrapped in mystery,
My life's a puzzling history.
I laugh at clouds that chase the sun,
While pondering questions, oh which one?

But still I smile, I learn to play,
In the quiet storm, I find my way.
Each moment fleeting, yet full of grace,
In the silence, I find my space.

Attempting to Grasp the Ether

Fingers reach for thoughts like air,
Grasping notions, they vanish, where?
Like soap bubbles, they drift and gleam,
What's this grand scheme? A fleeting dream.

An idea tickles, then slips away,
I chase after it, but it loves to play.
With jars of ideas, none fit quite right,
I scribble notes deep into the night.

A dance of nonsense, a waltz in disguise,
Curly fries or quantum ties?
A noodle of reason, a sprinkle of wit,
As chaos dances, I choose to sit.

So here I linger in this great chase,
Joy in the hunt, no need for a race.
In this absurdity, I take a bow,
As thoughts escape, I laugh somehow.

Shadows of a Fleeting Existence

Life's a shadow, flickering light,
I trip on thoughts both day and night.
A chase for meaning, but what's the score?
Is it all a play? Oh, what's in store?

With chuckles and giggles I ponder fate,
While searching for wisdom, I contemplate.
The toaster blinks, my breakfast awaits,
Yet here I stand, lost in debates.

Mirth in the chaos, a jester's grin,
What folly drives the thoughts within?
Are we the dreams or just the seams?
Stitching this life with borrowed themes.

So let's toast to shadows, laughter, and cheer,
In the moments we stumble, it all becomes clear.
Life's fleeting giggles are ours to embrace,
In this circus of bright, let's find our place.

www.ingramcontent.com/pod-product-compliance
Lightning Source LLC
Chambersburg PA
CBHW072147200426
43209CB00051B/814